Original title:
The Road to Meaning Is Under Construction

Copyright © 2025 Creative Arts Management OÜ
All rights reserved.

Author: Dexter Sullivan
ISBN HARDBACK: 978-1-80566-085-9
ISBN PAPERBACK: 978-1-80566-380-5

Lanes of Introspection and Insight

In the lane of thought, where ideas frolic,
Bubbles of doubt make the journey comical.
Traffic jams of worries shroud the clear view,
Yet laughter echoes, as truths come into view.

Detours of dreams lead to paths we forgot,
With funny signs warning of all that we've sought.
Laughter's the fuel, our guide on the way,
Navigating through quirks that brighten the day.

Construction Zone: Embracing Uncertainty

In the messy site of hopeful plans,
We build with laughter, using silly hands.
Wobbling cranes and a paint-splashed sky,
As we stumble together, we not just get by.

Hard hats on, it's a whimsical game,
In a sandbox of options, we're never the same.
With confusion as laughter's loyal cousin,
We dance through the chaos, hoping for reason.

Paving Over Past Footprints

With a shovel of chuckles, we bury the past,
As new tracks are laid, we outsmart the blast.
Old footprints are silly, like shoes on a dog,
We skip over memories, through mist and fog.

Each stone tells a joke, each crack has a tale,
Underneath laughter's veil, we set our sail.
Past puddles of sorrow, we shout with delight,
With every new layer, we shine ever bright.

Waypoints of Awareness

At waypoints of wisdom, the signs are all funny,
Sometimes it's serious, and sometimes it's punny.
A tumble of thoughts like squirrels on the run,
As we giggle at trips that seem never done.

Awareness is wobbly, like a bicycle's ride,
It laughs if you fall, in the journey, to glide.
With maps that are doodles and compasses askew,
We savor the twists, always ready for new.

Unseen Detours

I took a left when I should have gone right,
Now I'm lost in a taco stand's light.
They say life's a journey, with twists galore,
But I never thought it would come with a burrito store.

My GPS is taunting, with a snicker and grin,
'Rerouting, rerouting!' Oh where to begin?
A shortcut through the park, or perhaps the zoo?
Next thing I know, I'm knee-deep in goo!

Paths of Potential

Every path I explore seems to lead to a joke,
Like stepping on gum or tripping on smoke.
With potential so vast, yet chaos in tow,
I found a stray cat that decided to show.

Wandering further, I meet with a frog,
He croaks about fortune while sitting on logs.
'Leap into your dreams, don't just hop on by!',
But I'm still stuck here, covered in pie.

The Canvas of Creation

Painting my future with colors so bright,
But accidentally splattered my shirt—oh, what a sight!
Each brushstroke a step—if I can just stand,
Wait, is that blue or a spilled soda can?

With laughter like paint that just won't dry,
I scribble my plans, while letting out a sigh.
Creativity flows, though it's messy and wide,
At least I'm having fun while I take this ride!

Resilient Routes

If life's a dance, I've two left feet,
Yet I groove on ahead, can't accept defeat.
With bumps on my journey, I jiggle and sway,
Even when gravity tells me to stay.

Every slip is a trip that makes me laugh loud,
I bounce back with flair, shall I dance with this crowd?
Through mud and through puddles, I twirl with flair,
It's the messy, funny moments I truly declare!

Exploring Expansion

In a world chalked with options wide,
We hop on paths with laughter as our guide.
Maps are scribbled with doodles and cheer,
Two left feet dance, but we persevere.

Dirt paths lead us to ice cream stands,
With waffle cones in our unsteady hands.
We navigate puddles, splash in delight,
Each misstep a joy, each fall feels just right.

Signposts point in all sorts of ways,
One says 'frozen yogurt', the other 'fun craze'.
We ponder the choices, our heads in a spin,
For every new twist, we chuckle and grin.

Adventure awaits, with a wink and a nod,
We're builders of dreams, with laughter our facade.
Grab your map, but toss it in style,
For the journey's more fun if you go the wrong mile!

Carrying the Weight of Wonder

With backpacks full of dreams and snacks,
We trudge along, making silly tracks.
Crumbs of wisdom tumble with glee,
As we chase down a thought like it's a runaway bee.

Curiosity weighs like a ton,
But giggles erupt as we try to outrun.
Every question's a pebble stuffed in our pack,
We're treasure hunters, not looking to slack.

An umbrella's a hat in a sudden downpour,
And raindrops become our dance floor.
Oh what joy, in puddles we leap!
Finding joy in the messy, our hearts take a sweep.

With wonder in pockets and silliness near,
We carry our dreams like balloons filled with cheer.
So let's waddle and laugh on this bumpy pursuit,
For even the burdens can be underfoot loot!

Awakening from Stagnation

Sleepy thoughts begin to stir,
Like a cat with a sudden purr.
Chasing dreams that led astray,
Waking up in a funny way.

Time to shake the cold, hard ground,
Dance around without a sound.
Life's a circus, don't you see?
Clowns jump out, just let it be.

Paved with Questions

Look at signs, they twist and writhe,
Questions sprout like weeds, they thrive.
Where to go? Is it a trick?
Answer fast, or face the brick!

Queries land like bouncing balls,
Echoing in these empty halls.
Every thought's a merry dance,
Will I fall, or take a chance?

Carving Out Clarity

With a spoon, I dig for truth,
Crafting wisdom from my youth.
Chisels break, the pieces fly,
Is it clarity, or a pie?

Shapes emerge from stone so gray,
Laughter helps to clear the way.
Chisel more and laugh out loud,
Mistakes become my silly crown.

Endpoints of Existence

Where do we go when the map goes blank?
Follow the laughter, that's my prank.
Endpoints twist like funhouse mirrors,
Making wise men out of dreamers.

Counting socks instead of sheep,
In the dark, I laugh and leap.
Existence laughs in shades of jest,
Find your joy, forget the rest.

Walking the Undefined Path

I stumbled on a trail so wide,
Where lost socks and dreams abide.
Each footprint's filled with giggles and grins,
As I trip over the map to the bins.

Trees are laughing, birds take flight,
They wave their wings, say, 'What a sight!'
With every twist, I'm redefined,
In this tangled path, my thoughts unwind.

Crafting Meaning with Every Step.

I found a hammer and some glue,
To piece together my worldview.
With each step forward, I build anew,
A castle made of bright, odd shoe.

I mix confusion with a dash of flair,
Navigating life with no real care.
A blueprint scribbled in crayon bright,
For a structure that shifts in morning light.

Pathways of Purpose

I wandered down this quirky lane,
Where squirrels offer me champagne.
With every choice, I laugh and spin,
Should I chase my tail or the whim of a bin?

A compass made from jellybeans,
Guides me through these wacky scenes.
With each step, my worries melt,
In this zany world, I freely dealt.

Blueprint for Reflection

I sketched my thoughts on a paper plate,
And drew a mustache on my fate.
With a ruler bent in silly ways,
I measure joy in laughter plays.

My plans may wobble like a dog on skates,
As I ponder life between the states.
With a wink and nod, my map's complete,
In this funny chaos, I find my beat.

Foundations of Thought

In a world made of marshmallows, we tread,
Building castles on clouds, too much in our head.
Wobbling bricks of ice cream, a scoop here and there,
Wondering if life's just a big, fluffy lair.

With pickles for pillars and jellybeans for walls,
We sip lemonade dreams while gravity stalls.
A blueprint of giggles, in colors so bright,
Constructing our laughs under the soft twilight.

Nailing down beliefs with some tape and a glue,
A splash of confetti, oh what a view!
The laughter keeps echoing, it bounces around,
In this whimsical fortress, we're never profound.

Markers of Intent

Signposts made of donuts, directions unclear,
'Left at the sprinkles, then buy a cold beer.'
Navigating life with a fork as my guide,
Laughing at detours, with friends by my side.

Pavement of pudding, it squishes my shoes,
Following paths where I can't help but snooze.
Chasing the sunset on a unicycle ride,
With noodle-like gears, it's a whimsical glide.

Points of confusion, oh what a spectacle!
Frogs in top hats giving their best reticle.
Each turn a surprise, like a cake that's well-leavened,
Markers of intent, taking us to Heaven.

Shifting Directions

With compass in hand and a map upside down,
I wander through puddles dressed like a clown.
'Go straight until laughter, then turn right at fun,'
Each route leads to giggles, road work's never done.

My GPS sings like a parrot on loop,
'Veer left at the puppy, and join in the troop.'
Every step is a jiggle, a hop, and a bounce,
Each choice a confetti-filled, marvelous flounce.

Mapping out nonsense, the signs all misspoke,
Like riding a unicycle made out of smoke.
Yet somehow I find, in this comedic crawl,
That embracing the chaos has merits for all.

Gravel and Gold

On a highway of giggles, where gravel gets bold,
Stumbling on treasures, more precious than gold.
A tumble of chuckles, a dance with my shoes,
Finding joy in the detours, the mishaps, the blues.

Each bump a new story, each swerve a surprise,
Laughter like glitter, it sparkles and flies.
Digging in gravel, I uncover the fun,
A treasure map pointing to the warmth of the sun.

With friends by my side and the wind in my hair,
Life's road is a circus, no worries, no care.
So let's gather the laughs, let our hearts be so bold,
In the mix of the gravel, we'll find our bright gold.

The Work in Progress

In my life, I found blueprints,
With coffee stains and doodles.
My heart's like a DIY project,
Full of giggles and some poodles.

Tools are scattered everywhere,
And the hammer's missing too.
I think I'll skip the steps today,
Building castles out of glue.

Patches on my troubled dreams,
Like a quilt of wild desires.
Every stitch, a funny tale,
While I'm dodging life's flat tires.

Yet each mistake is just a laugh,
A stop sign with a grin.
I'm learning to embrace the flaws,
With a heartfelt chortle within.

Building the Bridge Within

I'm stacking bricks of laughter,
Each one shaped by silly jokes.
Cemented dreams hold it together,
While I'm dodging all the pokes.

A squirrel offered some advice,
As I wobbled near the edge.
"Use marshmallows, my friend!" he said,
And I thought, what a pledge!

The beams are swaying, oh dear me!
Maybe a rope swing is the call?
I swung too high, I lost my hat,
But man, did I have a ball!

Bridges made of bright balloons,
Dancing over every gap.
I'll skip the blueprints next time,
Just grab some snacks and take a nap!

The Construction Site of Self

At the site of my own being,
I'm the foreman with no clue.
Each piece I try to fit just right,
Ends up bent and askew.

I hired a talking crane,
But it only makes bad puns.
"Lift with your heart!" it gently quips,
As I fumble my work runs.

Caution tape around my dreams,
Warning: Enter at your risk!
With self-doubt as my hard hat,
Every whim feels like a brisk.

But a jackhammer of laughter roars,
As friends stop by to tease.
They say I'm a masterpiece,
Still drying out in the breeze.

Signs That Guide Us Home

I found some signs along my way,
Shaped like rubber chickens.
"Exit here to find your joy!"
Under neon, playful pickin's.

A "Detour" leads to ice cream shops,
Popsicles fly like meteors.
"Caution! Smiles ahead!" it reads,
With sprinkles labeled 'cure-all'.

I missed a turn, I slipped and fell,
Into a puddle – oh so grand!
But a sign yelled "Dance it out!"
I joined the rain with a shimmied hand.

Home is where the laughter lives,
With signs that twist and twine.
Follow arrows made of joy,
And you'll never lose your shine.

The Unfolding Map of Existence

In the attic lies a map, oh dear,
With coffee stains and crumbs from last year,
It leads to treasures, though they're unclear,
X marks the spot, or is it a beer?

A compass spins, we're going round,
Direction lost in the sights we've found,
We chase our tails, a circus profound,
Laughing at the place where wisdom's drowned.

Winding paths take twists and bends,
With each wrong turn, the fun transcends,
Our journey's more than just the ends,
It's the goofy signs that fate sends.

Lost in laughter, hearts take flight,
Navigating chaos feels just right,
With each step, we find delight,
In the quirky dance of day and night.

Barriers and Boundaries of Understanding

I built a wall to keep out fears,
But the flea market's drawn me near,
My logic's lost amid the cheers,
Who knew understanding could bring jeers?

A sign reads 'stop,' I just can't halt,
Should I climb over, or is that my fault?
With every question, fresh results,
Barriers turn into somersaults.

My neighbors speak in riddles, vague,
Do I need a manual to engage?
They laugh so hard, 'It's all the rage!'
Turns out learning's quite the vague stage.

Confusion reigns, oh what a mess,
But in humor, I find my dress,
With each blunder, I must confess,
I'm learning to love this great duress.

Footprints on the Fabric of Life

I stumbled through life's patchy quilt,
With mismatched socks and a hearty guilt,
Each footprint's shaped by jokes I've spilt,
In slapstick style, my fate was built.

A giant toe prints on the seam,
Tickling paths made of whipped cream,
And laughter weaves through every dream,
As I scuttle, wobbling like a beam.

Each tread's a tale, a laugh, a tease,
In puddles deep, I dance with ease,
While fabric stretches, I take my knees,
Grinning wide, I'm here to please.

So follow me, let's trip and slide,
With giggles grand and joy inside,
In this fabric life, let's run and bide,
Leaving footprints where laughter won't hide.

Detours That Define Us

I took a right when I should've turned,
Found a hot dog stand and my heart burned,
Detours teach, and oh how I've learned,
With mustard joy, my stomach churned.

Through winding streets and silly signs,
I discovered wisdom in bold designs,
I chuckled loud at all the pines,
Who knew the path had such fine lines?

Quick pit stops for ice cream cones,
Each scoop a laugh, and joy it hones,
In every loop, my inner groans,
Are traded in for silly tones.

Detours shape the lives we lead,
With every misstep, we plant a seed,
In humor found, we truly succeed,
As laughter grows, we're rich indeed.

Underneath the Tapestry of Time

Life's a quilt made of mismatched threads,
Sew it up with laughter, where the chaos spreads.
Stitch by stitch, we craft our own fate,
But don't ask the cat, she'll just contemplate.

Every patch holds a story, silly and grand,
Some are wild dreams, others—lost on the sand.
Whispers of wisdom in the knots we tie,
It's a jumbled mess, but we're all just trying to fly.

Constructions of the Soul

Building blocks of joy, we stack very high,
With a wobbly tower that scrapes the sky.
Blueprints made of doodles, scattered with care,
And let's not forget the rubber chicken there.

Some days it's a mansion, others a shed,
With paint that's still wet, ideas in our heads.
A construction site filled with hope and a laugh,
Just don't trip on the toolbox—it's half of the path.

Caution: Wisdom Ahead

Beware of the signs that giggle and tease,
A journey that leads to the land of 'sneeze!'
Each bump and pothole gives wisdom a shove,
And the GPS just tells you, 'Go have some fun!'

The road signs are quirky, the speed limits laugh,
As we drive into life's big, confused half.
Watch out for wisdom, it might take a spin,
Like a hamster on wheels, where's the start—where's the win?

Excavating Purpose in Shadows

Digging through shadows with a trowel and scoop,
What will we find? A lost rubber soup?
Treasures of laughter, some giggles of gold,
And the odd sock that's been hiding, so bold.

Each shovelful brings giggles and glee,
As we unearth the jokes that make us feel free.
A purpose built on puns, with laughter as guide,
Excavating joy, let's take it for a ride!

Pathways Paved with Questions

Why's the chicken cross the street?
To find answers—quite a feat!
But all it found was a doughnut shop,
Now it's in line, hoping to stop.

Wandering souls with puzzled minds,
Searching for signs of all kinds.
Maps of confusion in their hands,
They giggle at fate's strange plans.

Each turn a riddle, each path a jest,
In this quest for meaning, they jest.
With every step, a laugh or two,
Who knew searching would feel so new?

So here we are, lost but amused,
In life's big maze, perpetually confused.
Chasing knowledge like it's a game,
Is the journey worth it? Who's to blame?

Foundations of a Shifting Journey

Building blocks made of pure doubt,
Watch them wobble—will they fall out?
A silliness in every chunk,
As wisdom's toolbox goes just "clunk."

With shovels and buckets, they dig around,
Unearthing laughter from common ground.
The foundation shifts with each silly quake,
Even concrete knows when it's time to break.

The architects laugh, they wear hard hats,
Drawing blueprints of cats wearing spats.
Yet in the chaos, a plan must emerge,
To find joy's meaning—let laughter surge.

So here we lay pebbles of cheer,
Filling the cracks with great big jeers.
With every stumble and trip we'll laugh,
In this wobbly dance, we find our path.

Blueprints of Self-Discovery

They pulled out a blueprint, oh what a sight,
With squiggly lines and ideas so bright.
Plans for a castle, a ship, or a spire,
But ended up building a giant bonfire.

Instructions unclear—where to go next?
Follow your heart, you'll be perplexed.
With each building block turned upside down,
One wrong move, and you craft a clown.

The drafts are messy, the pencils are broke,
Yet laughter spills out with each silly poke.
Who knew self-discovery was a slapstick show?
With giggles and twists, we figure out "who?"

And so we scribble on empty space,
Paint outside the lines at an awkward pace.
Finding ourselves in this intricate dance,
Reveling in living—a whimsical chance!

Signs on the Endless Detour

A sign says, 'You are here,' but where's that?
Under the bridge? By a stray cat?
Each direction points in a crazy swirl,
Should I follow the arrows or just twirl?

Detour ahead! With a big red light,
Follow the path that feels just right.
Oh wait, it leads to a rubber duck
Now I'm sailing, how did I get stuck?

Traffic cones singing a silly song,
Making the road feel bright and wrong.
Should I detour to fun or stay lost?
In this revelry, what's the cost?

So here we march, with smiles so bright,
Finding joy even in the night.
With each swing of fate, the humor flows,
In this endless loop, who really knows?

Paving the Way with Dreams

I'm building a path with wishes so bright,
But lost my directions — oh what a sight!
With hammers and nails, I work every day,
But tripping on stones just takes me away.

There's laughter and giggles, a show under sun,
As I stumble around, thinking this is fun.
Each plank that I lay is a bit out of place,
Yet somehow I stumble into a new space.

I planned for a highway, but found a dirt track,
With squirrels as my crew, no turning back.
They say "Keep on building, we love the surprise!"
My blueprints are wild like a child's crazy tries.

Every brick that I place is a quirky new tale,
With ducks in hard hats and a friendly old snail.
So here in this chaos, I dance and I twirl,
Paving my way through this whimsical world.

Under Construction: A Life in Progress

Life's a big project, with tools spread about,
And I often get lost in what it's about.
With laughter as scaffolding, I build every day,
Hoping not to trip on my life's crazy play.

Blueprints are blurry, got coffee on plans,
While friends pass me wrenches and offer their hands.
"I swear I can fix it!" I confidently claim,
But end up installing my own foot in the frame.

Each task is a jigsaw, I'm missing some pieces,
With paint spills of passion, my progress increases.
A hammer's my gauge, my heart's on the line,
Constructing this life, I'm having a fine time.

One day this will flourish, I keep telling me,
Though right now I'm stuck in a pit of debris.
So pass me some laughs, and pass me some glue,
We'll build this together, me, you, and the zoo!

Fragments of a Journey

I've packed up my dreams in a suitcase of quirks,
And set off for somewhere where odd is what works.
With directions all mixed, I'm not sure where to go,
But that's what makes life such a delightful show.

There's laughter and chaos, I'm tripping on shoes,
In each twist and turn, I can't pick and choose.
A compass that spins like a top on its head,
I'm finding my way as I follow the lead.

With friends as my map, and joy as my guide,
We skip over puddles, we've nothing to hide.
So here's to the fragments, the stops along the route,
Each pause is a treasure, so let's give a hoot!

With pauses for giggles and snacks on the way,
My journey's a tapestry, bright as a ray.
So bring on the fragments, the stops and the starts—
This wild ride of life truly fills up our hearts.

Bridges to the Unknown

I'm building these bridges with sticks and with tape,
To cross over rivers of laughter and gape.
With duct tape for safety and dreams in my bag,
I hope that my bridge won't go down with a wag.

Each plank is a giggle, each rope is a cheer,
As I dangle above, my friends shout and jeer.
The unknown calls softly with a wink and a grin,
But if I take a wrong step, please don't let me spin!

I've got rubbery ducks acting as my crew,
They quack in approval whenever I do.
Construction's a party, it's silly and wild,
With giggles and laughter just like a young child.

So here's to the bridges, all wobbly and bright,
As we dance through the unknown under the moonlight.
Let's build and conjure, no fear of the fall,
For together we're strong, and we'll laugh through it all!

Uploading Inspiration

Wi-Fi's slow, the muse won't load,
Ideas buffering like an old road.
I hit refresh, but nothing's new,
Oh wait, a cat meme! That'll do.

Frantic typing, where's my flair?
Oops, I've just sent it to air.
My brain's a server that's down and out,
Maybe I'll just take a nap, no doubt.

I search for meaning on my phone,
But all I find is Google groan.
Inspiration's out, but that's okay,
I'll let my thoughts nap 'til tomorrow's day.

Songs of chaos play in the back,
My thoughts drift off on a snack attack.
Tomorrow's plans rest on my dreams,
But for now, it's just ice cream themes.

Emerging from the Fog

Woke up today, lost in a haze,
Thoughts swirling like a sitcom craze.
Where's my focus? Where's my spark?
Just my socks, and they miss the mark.

In the mist, I trip and laugh,
Oh look! A goose on my path.
"Excuse me, friend, do you have a clue?"
The goose just honks, as if to say, "Boo!"

Clouds of doubt dance all around,
Playing tag with thoughts I found.
But in the doom, a spark ignites,
I'll make a meme of my life's delights.

Fog lifts up, the sun sneaks through,
Eyes squinting at a sky so blue.
Maybe the world's not lost after all,
Just don't ask the goose—he'll make you fall!

Essential Excavation

Digging deep into my mind,
What treasures of wisdom can I find?
With a shovel made of giggles and glee,
I'll unearth the thoughts that chase me.

Oh look, a bone of a long-lost dream,
Why'd it get buried? Oh, how it screams!
A trowel of laughter clears the path,
Excavating joy, not aftermath.

I hit a gem, but what's this glow?
A glittery thought I used to know.
Polishing it with chuckles and cheer,
I'll hang it up on my wall, sincere.

Just remember, as you dig around,
Life's a comedy; humor's profound.
With each new find, let laughter reign,
In the mess of my mind, joy will remain.

Erosion of Expectations

I planned my day like a perfect cake,
But all I've got is a pancake flake.
My to-do list is now a buffet,
And the waiter's like, "Sorry, not today."

Life's a mountain, expectations tall,
But who knew gravity could make them fall?
With each topple, I giggle and say,
"Who needs plans when chaos is play?"

I wanted sunshine, got a drizzle instead,
But look, a rainbow—my worries fled.
So I dance in puddles, splash my doubts,
Finding joy in the unexpected routes.

Erosion might reshape the whole scene,
But change is just life's way to glean.
So raise a glass to twists and turns,
In the comedy of life, our spirit burns.

The Architecture of Ambivalence

Wobbly bridges made of doubt,
Balancing visions, in and out.
Plans all tangled in a pile,
Blueprints that just make you smile.

Nailing hopes to walls of dreams,
A comedy of scheming teams.
Do we want window views or bricks?
Maybe just some funny tricks!

Two doors open, which to choose?
Flip a coin, you're bound to lose.
Sketches laughing at the strain,
In this house of silly brain.

Foundations shake, a playful jest,
Wonky beams, an architect's quest.
Here's to all the drafts that fail,
Building laughter without a bail.

Layers of Experience

Onion skins of trials we peel,
Each layer reveals a new deal.
Wisdom wrapped in quirky guise,
Where truth and jest intertwine and rise.

Spices of joy, a dash of woe,
Mix it up, let your heart show.
Recipes made with laughter's blend,
Who knew our messes can still mend?

A taste of wisdom, a pinch of zest,
Whisking through life's ongoing jest.
Serve it warm with a twist of fate,
Bon appétit, don't be late!

We stir the pot with silly flair,
Every drop a moment to share.
Layers of love, a hint of cheer,
Here's to cooking up a great year!

Fractured Landscapes

Mountains of mishaps in the range,
Viewing life through a funny change.
Cracks in logic, valleys of fun,
Where reason's lost, imagination's won.

A river flows with comic grace,
Bouncing rocks in a silly race.
Cacti smile with prickly cheer,
Waving at all who wander near.

Deserts of doubt, oases of glee,
Sipping joy beneath a quirky tree.
Fields of laughter, crops growing wild,
Harvesting giggles, nature's child.

These landscapes bend with laughter's hand,
Painting the chaos, it's all unplanned.
A fractured world, a jigsaw piece,
Finding humor brings sweet release.

Waystations of Wisdom

Pit stops in a funny place,
Sipping coffee, sharing grace.
Signposts winking, urging halt,
Relishing life's comical vault.

Maps all tangled, paths entwine,
Asking strangers, "What's the line?"
Laughing gas at each station stall,
Writing down the tales of all.

Bumpy rides on a wobbly bus,
Each bump a laugh, no room for fuss.
Waystations filled with quirks to see,
Collecting smiles, that's the key!

Hitchhikers' joy in every detour,
Strange adventures knocking at your door.
So grab the giggles, don't forget,
In this journey, joy's our best bet!

Cementing Connections

Slips and trips upon the dust,
Friends I find in mud, we trust.
Laughter echoes, spirits blend,
With each stumble, new bonds mend.

Pavement dreams in hot asphalt,
Who knew chaos could be our vault?
Each mix-up turns into a joke,
Our hearts dance as friendships stoke.

Ripple Effect of Choices

Choose a snack, then drop a fry,
Chaos unfolds; oh my, oh my!
One small bite leads to a wave,
Tummy aches but laughter saves.

Paths diverge from bites we take,
Should I eat the cake or bake?
Each decision twists and twirls,
Life's a laugh, it swirls and swirls.

Uncharted Territories

Maps are fun, but who needs those?
Let's explore where wild wind blows.
Lost in laughter, not in fear,
Each wrong turn brings friends near.

With every bump on this weird ride,
We gather joy, put doubt aside.
Adventure calls with silly cheer,
Embrace each twist, my dear, my dear.

Hard Hats and Heartbeats

Hard hats on, we strut like kings,
Under construction, joy it brings.
Tools in hand, we whistle loud,
Building hope, we're feeling proud.

Safety first? Well maybe not!
Falling laughs, we hit the spot.
Every clatter, every fall,
Adds a giggle, we stand tall.

Beyond the Detour Signs

I took a path that made no sense,
With every turn, I lost my chance.
GPS said, 'You're on the way,'
But all I found was a goat ballet.

Traffic cones wore silly hats,
Pointing to where I should relax.
A sign said, 'Bump Ahead!' I zipped,
And suddenly, my coffee tipped!

I waved to birds that looked bemused,
Thought perhaps I'd just been confused.
A squirrel popped out, gave me a grin,
And offered nuts for my next spin.

But laughter sparkled in the air,
Like confetti tossed without a care.
Though detours seem to steal the show,
They lead to tales we'll love to show.

Foundations of an Evolving Heart

I laid my bricks with sticky glue,
Thinking of all the things I'd do.
My heart, a house with windows wide,
But squirrels called dibs! They moved inside.

I tried to paint all walls in red,
But ended up with blue instead.
Each stroke a giggle, every hue,
Transformed my fortress – who knew?

Blueprints scattered all around,
An architect who loved to clown.
A focus group of laughing cats,
Gave feedback through their casual chats.

I danced on floors I hadn't made,
While shadows of my plans did fade.
Yet joy sprouted where doubts once lay,
Foundations shift, but fun must stay.

The Unfinished Journey Within

I packed my bags for a great trip,
With mismatched socks and a banana slip.
Thought I'd find the meaning of it all,
But I just tripped on an unseen wall.

I wandered through a maze of thoughts,
Each corner met with quirky dots.
A sign said, 'Left or right, who knows?'
A llama winked; oh, how it glows!

An inner voice, like peanut butter,
Stuck on questions that made me stutter.
'Why did you pack that oddball spoon?'
'It's for the soup of the afternoon!'

The journey's long, but that's okay,
With silly clues leading the way.
Each step a giggle, a dance, a spin,
An unfinished map to the grin within.

Blueprints of Hope in Progress

I laid my plans on a back porch chair,
With lemonade while without a care.
Sketches of dreams adorned my page,
   A workspace turned into a stage.

My hammer's squeaking a tune so sweet,
   Dancing eyes with shuffle of feet.
I built a swing from scattered thoughts,
  Pretending wisdom can't be bought.

Plans grew wild like a garden here,
With roses that laughed and ate a beer.
Every wall, a story told in jest,
Like lessons learned, they came to rest.

If blueprints change, then let them bend,
For humor's laughter will always send.
A house of joy is made to grow,
With hopes and dreams that steal the show.

Half-Built Destinations

In a land where signposts point the wrong way,
People wander, lost, in yesterday's play.
Each path a riddle, like socks in the wash,
They trip on their thoughts with a foolish bosh.

Up ahead, a bridge that leads to nowhere,
With a view of a ditch and a bird in despair.
Tourists take selfies with a fence post so proud,
Declaring they've found what no one has vowed.

There's a map that suggests some grand fate,
But the compass spins wildly, it just can't relate.
When life hands you lemons, make lemonade weird,
Serving up laughter, the joy we all cheered.

So dance in the dust, on this path unclear,
Each stumble a giggle, each turn brings a cheer.
If you can't find the answer, just make it a joke,
And take all your missteps with a spirit bespoke.

The Quest for Clarity

With a shovel for thinking, they dig through the haze,
Uncovering treasures, in puzzling ways.
Yet every gold coin is tangled with threads,
Of thoughts that run wild like a clown in their beds.

A checklist of goals pinned high on the wall,
But the footnotes are checkered, it's a carnival ball.
They juggle their dreams in a circus of doubt,
And tumble through laughter, figuring it out.

They find a wise owl, who's really just sage,
Spouting odd riddles from a whimsical age.
His advice: wear shoes that are mismatched and loud,
For clarity's lost in a wobbly crowd.

Yet through all the chaos, they laugh and they play,
Embracing the mess is the best kind of way.
For every great quest isn't just a straight line,
But a comedy act where the punchlines all shine.

Building Blocks of Being

They stack up their colors, a vibrant array,
With blocks that are wobbly, yet here they stay.
A purple one's giggling, a green one's a clown,
In this building of beings, they never frown.

Each piece tells a story, a wild little tale,
Of marshmallow dreams and a pickle-based trail.
They trip on their laughter, with glue on their hands,
As they craft a fine castle of crumbly sands.

With blueprints that shift like the wind on a kite,
They measure their hopes with a ruler of light.
Dripping with chaos, these blocks play the game,
While the architect snickers, "We're all a bit lame!"

But in this grand building of whoever they'll be,
Every tumble is glorious, every fall is free.
For the blocks may be scattered, and the plans may be weird,
But the joy in creation is exactly what's cheered.

Asphalt and Ambiguity

They laid down the pavement, but forgot where it led,
With potholes of options, and a skip of dread.
Ambiguity festers like gum on the heel,
As they shuffle through life with a slapstick appeal.

With signs that all read, "This way to the fun!"
But every direction leads back to square one.
Detours are plenty, like strippers of fate,
And when they get close, they find they're too late.

A map drawn in crayon, by a child's wild hand,
Turns navigation into a sleight-of-hand stand.
"Is that a cafe or a mysterious swamp?"
Each choice is a gamble, each step brings a chomp.

So they dance on the asphalt, all twisted and bent,
Making lemonade from all the time that they spent.
With giggles and grumbles, they wander along,
In a world full of asphalt, where chaos is song.

Journeys Yet Untold

I set out on a quest, so bright,
With snacks and tunes, oh what a sight.
But then I took a wrong turn, it seems,
Now I'm lost in a land of llamas and dreams.

A sign reads, 'Go left for the best snack!'
But I wandered right, and that's a fact.
I met a penguin who gave me advice,
'Life's just a dance, don't think twice!'

With every twist, a giggle grew,
Adventures unexpected, all brand new.
I tripped on a rock, said, 'Whoa, that's bold!'
But laughter's the treasure, yet to be sold.

So here I am, with a smile so wide,
Finding joy while I learn to glide.
Each misstep's a lesson, so clear and bright,
This journey's a riot, what a delight!

Signposts of Insight

I stumbled on signs that danced and spun,
Pointing to wisdom, or just some fun.
'Go straight for the donuts, take a right for cheer,'
But the donuts were gone, oh dear, oh dear!

A sign post wobbled, with humor so bold,
'Ask a goat for advice, he's wise, I'm told.'
I found a goat, looking quite sage,
But all he said was, 'Turn to the page!'

So I flipped through life like a curious chap,
Chasing the clues like they're in a map.
Each arrow a chuckle, each step a grin,
Making sense of nonsense is where I begin.

As I wander down paths absurd and bright,
Every mishap becomes pure delight.
With giggles and wiggles, I dance along,
Following signposts to laughter's sweet song!

The Unfinished Map

My map is a puzzle, all jumbled and torn,
With dog legs and squiggles since the day I was born.
A squiggle to coffee, a loop to a song,
Who needs directions when you're feeling so strong?

X marks the spot, or was it a tree?
One thing is certain, it won't guide me.
I drew a big heart in the middle of town,
Stopped to lounge, won't let fun drown.

Each corner I turn, a surprise does await,
Like socks in the dryer that beckon me late.
A wink from a squirrel, a nod from a bee,
Nature's confetti, how sweet it can be!

So I wander along, with laughter my map,
In a world full of wonders, I'm never in a trap.
With each twist and turn, my spirit takes flight,
An unfinished journey, but oh, what a sight!

Detours to Discovery

I planned a straight path to wisdom and truth,
But ended up lost, as they say in my youth.
A detour appeared, like a mirage in sand,
Led me to giggles, a rubber band band.

Each bend in the road brought curious sights,
Like dancing cucumbers in dazzling lights.
They said, 'Join us, we're forming a crew,'
Made a salad of laughs, my oh, how we grew!

Rerouting my travels, I found such delight,
In places where laughter can take to flight.
Each stumble a riddle, each fall just a score,
Turns out my journey is less about the lore.

So here's to the detours, the trips we don't plan,
To the zany adventures where we all can ran.
For in every wrong turn, there's giggles to find,
Life's a whimsical ride, so curious and kind!

Roadwork Ahead: Options and Obstacles

Traffic cones dance in a line,
While pickup trucks sip their wine.
Detours twist like a curly fry,
Guess we'll find out as we drive by.

Potholes deeper than my dreams,
Warning signs with funny themes.
Construction crews having a ball,
Juggling plans that seem to stall.

Lanes merge with an awkward flair,
Waving flags like we don't care.
Weaving through this wacky maze,
Laughing at the road's delays.

So, grab your map and your cheer,
Adventure's out there, never fear!
With each bump, we'll learn a thing,
Finding joy in what life can bring.

Whispers Beneath the Asphalt

The ground speaks softly, with a sigh,
As nature beneath starts to pry.
Cracks open like a frosty brew,
Who knew the earth had jokes, too?

Concrete dreams are hard to break,
But whispers rise like a cupcake.
See how gravel tries to rhyme,
Just don't let it waste your time!

Underneath those parking lots,
Lies a treasure of secret thoughts.
Beneath the hum of shifting cars,
Fables slumber, wishing on stars.

So listen close, there's much to hear,
Makes you chuckle, brings you cheer.
In every crack and every creak,
Funny stories wait to speak.

Charting Unknown Territories

Maps are scribbled, paths unclear,
A compass spins with frosty cheer.
Lost in laughter, we forge ahead,
Dropped our GPS, but not our thread.

Uneven trails and clumsy marks,
Hoping to dodge those pesky sharks.
Each wrong turn leads to delight,
As we dance beneath the moonlight.

Google Maps took a coffee break,
Now we're left with jokes to make.
Through the bushes, we'll find a prize,
Or at least some frogs in disguise.

So here's to paths we never planned,
With silly signs we understand.
In every twist, a chuckle grows,
Adventurers, together, the journey flows.

Vision Under Renewal

With goggles on, we squint and glance,
To see the future in a dance.
Vision boards made of tape and glue,
Fixing dreams, just me and you.

Repainted signs with messages bold,
Whispers of wisdom, tales retold.
A blueprint to make us laugh and play,
As we sketch our dreams on a sunny day.

Fences sway, bowing to grace,
Even traffic lights join the race.
In every glitch, a giggle rolls,
Chasing sunsets, catching goals.

So shine like asphalt, smooth and bright,
With humor as our guiding light.
Renewal brings a flurry of cheer,
On this wild ride, we persevere.

Uncharted Roads of Reflection

With a map upside down, I roam,
Each turn a surprise, far from home.
Potholes giggle, they trip my feet,
And whispers of wisdom come from the street.

I ask for directions, a squirrel just stares,
I pretend he knows, combing my hairs.
Puddles reflect my puzzled face,
Like funhouse mirrors, all over the place.

Left or right? Oh, what a delight!
Halfway to nowhere, it feels just right.
I paint my own path, with joy not dread,
Who knows where I'll end up? - I'll follow my head.

Gravel and Grace: A Traveler's Tale

Stumbling on gravel, my feet tap dance,
Every pebble feels like a chance.
With my suitcase full of mismatched socks,
I waddle along, creating new blocks.

I've got snacks for a marathon quest,
Crumbs on my shirt, I look like a mess.
But laughter's my guide, it lights up the day,
Guess there's merit in going astray.

A signpost stands, blank as a wall,
I flip it for fun, hoping it calls.
If life's an adventure, then here's my flair,
Navigating chaos, without a care.

Building Bridges to the Heart

I'm crafting a bridge with spaghetti strands,
Silly ideas, born from two hands.
With each noodle, I stretch and sway,
Hoping my feelings won't slip away.

A tug on the strands, oh what a sound!
Explosive giggles bounce all around.
A glue stick for love, what a great tool,
We'll stick together, it's totally cool.

I'll build a fort of laughter and fun,
With crow's feet hints of the sun.
In this construction zone, I'll settle down,
With jokes as my crown, I'll wear a big frown!

Navigating a Landscape of Intent

On a map of thoughts, I draw little hearts,
Navigating through life, where silliness starts.
With crayons in hand, I sketch my fate,
Chasing my dreams, isn't it great?

Intentions may wobble like jelly on toast,
But adding a smile is what I love most.
If purpose is fickle, let's wiggle and shout,
Dance through the mishaps, that's what it's about.

So here's my compass, it spins and it twirls,
Leading me through these adventurous swirls.
In the landscape of life, I'll bounce and I'll glide,
Finding the path where joy and fun abide.

Treads of Time

With each step, I trip and fall,
My shoes are tied, but I can't recall.
The clock's a friend, yet a foe in disguise,
Ticking away as my cat just sighs.

Road signs point to mysteries vast,
Which way to go? I'm aghast!
A map in my pocket, yet lost as could be,
Following squirrels, they seem so free!

People rush by, all in a hurry,
While I wander, lost in my flurry.
They say it's a journey, a marvelous quest,
But my shoes are screaming, "Just take a rest!"

Each puddle's a pit stop for my shoes to take bath,
I dance like a clown, oh, what a laugh!
Every bump on the path, with grace I encounter,
No GPS needed for my grand misadventure.

Weaving Through the Wilderness

In the woods where wild things thrive,
I take a step, and a twig comes alive.
My path covered in leaves, a spiky surprise,
Nature giggles as I try to devise.

A squirrel requests a selfie, quite bold,
My camera's not ready, but hey, let's be sold!
I trip on a root, my balance is toast,
Yet here in the wild, I'm the laughing host.

Rabbits hop by, showing off their tricks,
While I fumble and stumble, a comedy fix.
They say "keep it real!" as I fall on my face,
This wilderness stroll—a comedic grace!

With every misstep, I chuckle aloud,
For life's little moments should never be bowed.
So here's to the wild, absurd and divine,
For in this chaos, I'll always be fine.

Paths Frayed and Worn

My sneakers are old, soles barely intact,
They squeak and they squawk, now that's a fact!
With each step on this frayed-out trail,
I think of a train—wait, where's my mail?

Muddy footprints tell stories of yore,
Spaghetti-sauce stains from lunch, oh, what a chore!
I navigate like a deer with no grace,
Each stumble a dance, just a different pace.

A signpost reads "detour" but I'm on the wrong path,
While ants hold a meeting, conducting their math.
"Hey, push that pebble!" one ant shouts in delight,
"Oh no, my shoes! What a terrible sight!"

So I laugh at the journey, a circus it seems,
With paths that are frayed, but filled with dreams.
Each misstep's a punchline, a reason to smile,
For in this adventure, I'll stay for a while.

Beneath the Surface of Struggle

Trekking through life, dodging each snag,
I wave at confusion, with a big ol' brag.
Every twist and turn, a tale in the sky,
As clouds make faces that seem to reply.

I wrestle with troubles, a comical fight,
Juggling my snacks under dim little light.
The snacks hit the ground—oh, what a loss!
A raccoon munches, his laughter embossed.

I dive deep inside, where the chuckles reside,
Finding joy in the chaos, my whimsical guide.
For every great struggle, a punchline awaits,
Wrapped in the laughter that life generates.

So here's to the journeys, the silly and grand,
Where fun and adventure seem always close at hand.
With each little stumble, we find some more cheer,
Dance through the struggles, let's give them a cheer!

Navigating the Uncertain

Lost my map, and I'm not a fan,
My GPS thinks it knows my plan.
Ran a circle, oh what a sight,
My coffee's gone, but my hopes are bright.

Every turn feels like a joke,
Silly signs, that one said 'Yolk.'
Traffic cones dance in the sun,
I laugh at what I've yet to run.

Mice on bikes are racing through,
Just my luck, it's my cue!
Who knew that life's a wild ride?
With squirrels cheering from the side.

So here I go, no rules to bind,
Like a child playing hide and find.
With every twist, I lose my frown,
Just a traveler in a strange town.

Toll Booths of Truth

Pulled up to a booth today,
A friendly face said 'Pay your way!'
Coins in hand, with a grin so wide,
Turns out, the truth's a bumpy ride.

"Do you really want to know?" she said,
As I searched for coins instead of dread.
Hoping for lollipops, maybe some fun,
But it seems my journey just begun.

One lane for honesty, the other for lies,
Guess which one led to my surprise?
"I only take cards," the lady winked,
And off I went, rather perplexed, I blinked.

A toll for each truth, how absurd!
"Next time, bring snacks," I heard her purr.
So I drive on, with a shake of my head,
Life's just a game, here's where I tread.

Sketches of Self-Discovery

With crayons out and a giant sheet,
I scribble dreams beneath my feet.
A giraffe wearing socks by the line,
What's life without a little design?

I paint my trials, they're rather crude,
Splash of laughter, a dash of mood.
Cartwheeling through doubts and fears,
Each sketch brings more to my cheers.

Then came a cat, purple and strange,
"Why so serious?" it said, "Let's change!"
So I dip my brush in a pot of joy,
Draw a big rainbow, oh boy, oh boy!

Every sketch a tiny clue,
Of who I am and what is true.
With crayons in hand, I'm feeling bold,
In this wild art, my heart unfolds.

Horizons of Hope

Woke up today with socks that don't match,
Dreams of greatness take me to scratch.
With cereal afloat like tiny boats,
I find my hope on breakfast notes.

The toaster pops, a burnt delight,
It's a sign I'm meant to take flight.
With every bite, I smile and cheer,
The horizon's clearer with each passing year.

Sunsets dance in shades of fun,
Chasing laughter, on the run.
A kite that flew but met a tree,
Still holds a wish, just wait and see.

So let's trip in flip-flops, no shoes to tie,
Embracing the whimsy as we touch the sky.
Every stumble just adds to the charm,
Horizons of hope, they're all my arm.

Signs Along the Way

Every sign around here points to lunch,
They say snacks lead to wisdom, what a hunch!
A detour for coffee? That's just my style,
This path is chaotic, but oh, so worthwhile!

A post-it note warns, 'Beware of the ducks!'
As if feathery friends could cause real bad luck!
Traffic cones dance like they're at a fair,
I guess work zones can also show flair!

A billboard claims, 'Happiness is a jog,'
But I'm more a fan of a lazy dog!
So I'll stroll in style, with snacks I can munch,
While dreaming of a banquet—oh, what a brunch!

With each laugh, the path feels less surreal,
These signs make me ponder—what's the big deal?
Maybe the bumps just prepare us for glee,
As I trip on my shoelace, 'Oops!' That's just me!

Widening Perspectives

My glasses broke, but hey, what a view!
My path looks like a circus, and I'm the new crew!
This wide lens of life? All askew and hee-haw,
Who knew that falling could give me a flaw?

Open your mind, they say, with a twist!
But I'm tripping on thoughts that I thought I'd missed.
A buffet of ideas? Where do I start?
With noodle soup wisdom—now that's high art!

A cat on the corner gives me some sass,
"Keep your eyes on the prize, don't let life pass!"
But that prize looks like tuna, I'll take a bite,
And figure it out—maybe later tonight!

So I gather my snacks, and widen my grin,
Who knew perspective could come with a spin?
With each funny stumble, I take it in stride,
Embracing the chaos, my quirky joyride!

The Intersection of Dreams

At the corner of wishful and whacky today,
A sign says, 'Dare to dream? Just hop on the grey!'
I blink, and I see a parade of old socks,
Leading their dance to the rhythm of clocks!

There's confusion in traffic with wishes and hopes,
As we navigate life like it's tug-of-war ropes.
But those singing pigeons? They steal the show,
With their tap-dance routine, oh, how they glow!

A rubber duck floats by with a wink and a quack,
"Life's better with laughs, so don't hold back!"
I hop on my dreams, like they're merry-go-rounds,
Spinning in joy where true magic abounds!

So here's to the crossroads, however absurd,
With each quirky turn, I shall not be deterred!
For at this intersection, I'm free to explore,
With giggles and dreams, I'll always want more!

Pilgrimage of Possibilities

Packing my bags with snacks and some socks,
My journey begins—let's find some odd blocks!
I'm marching for giggles, and fun's on the list,
With a map made of candy, you'll get my gist!

Every step on this quest is wrapped in delight,
Chasing squirrels who skitter, what a silly sight!
They're leading me onward, oh, wait, where'd they go?
On this pilgrimage, I'm just putting on a show!

The golden arches beckon, calling my name,
But it's more about fries than the pilgrimage fame!
With ketchup rivers and smiles all around,
This journey of snacks is where joy can be found!

So, let's celebrate whims, and each little bump,
For this pilgrimage's charm is the heart of the jump!
With laughter as my compass, I'll venture anew,
Embracing all wonders, forever in view!

Intersection of Ideas

At the corner of thought and whim,
Ideas collide; it's a joyful brim.
With laughter and sighs, they twist and shout,
Who knew the brain could branch out so stout?

A parade of concepts, dancing around,
Tripping on logic, they fall on the ground.
Each bright notion, a balloon on a string,
Floating together, what chaos they bring!

Jokes made of puns bounce off the walls,
While wisdom in sneakers trips and falls.
The bright sparks of thought, a flickering show,
In this zany circus, ideas overflow!

So gather your thoughts, let's mix and match,
In this bustling hub, there's no need to catch.
Just ride the wave of a quirky idea,
And laugh at the puzzle, while sipping your soda!

Footsteps in Transition

Once a confident stride, now a shuffle and skip,
Searching for meaning, I trip on my lip.
Each step a riddle, a hopscotch of fate,
With every misstep, I giggle, not hate.

Eager to leap through a puddle of dreams,
I splash through confusion, or so it seems.
Laughing at footprints, they dance out of line,
A comedic parade; now isn't that fine?

With grapefruits for shoes, I waddle along,
Believing in jingles of cheerful old songs.
I'm lost in the fun of this awkward parade,
Where charm is the compass, and joy is the shade!

In this whimsical journey, we all coexist,
With a wink and a grin, we can't help resist.
So let's embrace the mishaps we find,
And treat every oops like a gift for the mind!

Dusty Trails to Tomorrow

These worn-out paths lead to nowhere fast,
A twist and a turn, I'm stuck in the past.
With dust on my shoes, and a joke on my tongue,
I travel the trail where the absurd is sung.

Tomorrow's a mystery wrapped up in jest,
I trip over futures; I thought they were best.
With giggles and snorts, I plow through the grime,
Each hiccup is hilarious; it's all part of the climb!

I've seen turtles race with the speed of a sloth,
And rabbits who knit with a tea-drinking froth.
In this land of oddities, laughter is gold,
And stories of quirks are the treasures we hold!

So pack up your worries, and join in the spree,
With every misstep, you'll find glee is key.
Embrace the absurd, let your spirit fly,
On these dusty trails, together we'll sigh!

Reconstructing Belief

With a hammer of hope and a bunch of good puns,
I'm building a castle, with all of my runs.
Nailing down doubts while giggling with glee,
It's a whimsical structure, just wait and see!

Each block is a notion, quirky and bright,
A tower of laughter, reaching new heights.
The windows are doubts that I polish with care,
And the roof, it's made of my wildest dare!

With scaffolding dreams, I'll hoist up the fun,
Taking shortcuts to laughter, no need to outrun.
As I stand on this ledge of my jumbled designs,
I find that my blueprints have thousands of signs!

So step inside my belief under construction,
Where whimsy and wonder dance in conjunction.
Let's build with our quirks, and each bumble we share,
In this joyful endeavor, there's magic in the air!

www.ingramcontent.com/pod-product-compliance
Lightning Source LLC
Chambersburg PA
CBHW071852160426
43209CB00003B/527